THE VICTORIAN GARDENER

Caroline Ikin

SHIRE PUBLICATIONS

Published in Great Britain in 2014 by Shire Publications Ltd, PO Box 883, Oxford, OX1 9PL, UK.

PO Box 3985, New York, NY 10185-3985, USA.

E-mail: shire@shirebooks.co.uk www.shirebooks.co.uk

A CIP catalogue record for this book is available from the British Library.

Shire Library no. 780. ISBN-13: 978 0 74781 327 9

Designed by Tony Truscott Designs, Sussex, UK and typeset in Perpetua and Gill Sans.

Cover design & photography by Peter Ashley; back cover detail: Victorian scrapbook item (author's collection).

Printed in China through Worldprint Ltd.

14 15 16 17 18 10 9 8 7 6 5 4 3 2 1

TITLE PAGE IMAGE

With no welfare state to provide for them, many gardeners were obliged to work on into old age.

CONTENTS PAGE IMAGE

A group of gardeners with the tools of their trade, *c.* 1910.

ACKNOWLEDGEMENTS

My thanks to Philip Norman at the Garden Museum for all his help with the illustrations, to Rebecca Graham at Nymans, to Shirley Courtney at Writtle College, and to Linda Cousins for her discerning comments on the text.

I would like to thank the following people who have allowed me to use illustrations:

Andrea Jones/Garden Exposures Picture Library, page 32 (bottom); Bridgeman Art Library, page 48; National Portrait Gallery, page 20 (top); reproduced with the kind permission of the Board of Trustees of the Royal Botanic Gardens, Kew (KGU/1/9/3/262), page 42; RHS Images, page 54; Writtle College, page 36.

All other images courtesy of the Garden Museum.

CONTENTS

INTRODUCTION

Horticultural skills were passed down through the generations, with the garden boy learning his trade from the experience of older gardeners.

THE VICTORIAN ERA, and the subsequent years up to the outbreak of the First World War, were a time of great social change. The rise of the middle classes and the increasing freedom enjoyed by women had a huge impact on the gardening profession, and advancements in science and technology brought increased status to horticulture. By the mid-nineteenth century gardening was a flourishing profession. Britain was enjoying peacetime prosperity, with low taxes and low inflation, and many landowners were making money from mineral extraction on their land or by investment in the new railways. Gardens were being created, improved and expanded across the country and demand for gardeners was high. The need for outdoor staff was matched by the increasing numbers of workers employed indoors, with Victorian households run with exacting precision by an army of domestic servants.

The head gardener ranked professionally alongside the butler, but although he was necessarily better educated and undertook a more rigorous training he was paid substantially less. The indoor and outdoor servants were managed separately and generally segregated, with only the head gardener having any need to cross the threshold of the house. The cook was reliant on the head gardener to provide produce for the kitchen, and a good working relationship was required to ensure that culinary needs were met, with fruit and vegetables arriving as expected and in the necessary quantities. The provision of flowers for the house would also be carefully arranged between the head gardener and the housekeeper to minimise the risk of a member of the family meeting a servant unexpectedly or encountering a bloom past its prime.

The number of servants employed in private service, both indoors and outdoors, peaked in 1871. The agricultural depression of the 1880s prompted cutbacks in staffing, as incomes from land plummeted, and the outbreak of the First World War signalled the end of the heyday of domestic service. Not only was the amount of labour available reduced by the demands of war, but post-war taxation crippled many aristocratic households and changing social attitudes resulted in an unwillingness of the working classes to return to the days of subservience. After the war, this combination of high taxes and labour shortages resulted in many large estates being sold, with gardens scaled back or neglected, glasshouses destroyed and costly bedding schemes abandoned. The skills of generations of gardeners were lost in the conflict, and the pre-war extravagance that had created so many gardens was replaced by the post-war austerity of their decline. This, combined with the expansion of the middle classes living in smaller country houses and suburban villas, created a new kind of gardener. Many amateur gardeners were now, through choice or necessity, able to manage their own gardens, assisted by gardening manuals and labour-saving devices such as the lawnmower. The gardener as a servant had been displaced, and the gardening profession began to take on its modern characteristics.

The head gardener at Wardown Park near Luton, photographed in 1906, presided over work in the garden departments. His professional ranking was akin to that of the butler, who managed the house staff.

A CAREER IN GARDENING

GARDENING was regarded as a respectable profession, with good opportunities for advancement for a hard-working young man intent on self-improvement. Apprenticeships enabled the passing-on of practical skills from experienced gardeners, and books and manuals facilitated private study. A would-be gardener had to take charge of his own career, securing funding for his apprentice fee, identifying the best gardens in which to learn his trade, being willing to travel around the country to gain experience, and making contact with influential gardeners who might provide a step up the ladder of advancement. After a hard day at work, the ambitious young gardener's labours were not over: he might spend the evening studying books on botany, geometry and plant physiology, or attending lectures on natural history.

A gardener working on a private estate was entering a profession with a hierarchy just as stringent as that found in domestic service. The head gardener was in charge of the gardeners in the same way that the butler directed the indoor staff, each commanding the respect and obedience of his workforce. At the bottom of the career ladder was the garden boy, who, at around twelve years of age and with a decent education, was expected to undertake the most menial of garden tasks, such as washing pots, picking slugs from plants and scaring birds. After around a year of service, the garden boy would be taught how to prick out seedlings and tie in wall plants, and would be engaged in repetitive tasks such as these, gaining basic skills around the garden and practising horticultural techniques.

At sixteen years of age, a boy could progress to become an under-gardener, getting a good grounding in all departments of the garden and learning technical skills from his superiors. At this point, an ambitious young gardener might apply for a position in a different garden to gain a broad range of skills and experience before moving on to become a journeyman gardener.

Journeymen had a peripatetic working life, moving from garden to garden to develop skills in all areas of horticulture. Advancement was self-motivated and it was up to the individual to identify suitable gardens in which to seek employment. A renowned head gardener could offer high-quality training

Opposite:
Many enthusiasts built their own orchid houses to display their collections, as in this photograph from c. 1910.

The most menial and unskilled of garden jobs were given to the garden boy, often necessitating anti-social working hours. This illustration from 1887 shows a boy removing slugs at night by lamplight.

and bestow recommendations for advancement, but he would be looking for only the most ambitious and talented young gardeners to work under him. A journeyman might also seek work in a nursery establishment to learn propagation skills and to become familiar with the cultivation of newly introduced plants, and working in different parts of the country would provide experience of various growing conditions and the merits of different types of soil and climate.

Journeymen would learn from experienced gardeners but would also be expected to undertake considerable study from books and manuals in the evening, supplementing their horticultural knowledge with the study of book-keeping, foreign languages, technical drawing, natural history and chemistry. Once all the necessary skills had been learned, a gardener could apply for a position as a foreman, leading one of the

Through apprenticeships, young gardeners could learn horticultural skills from experienced gardeners. The quality of their training depended on the knowledge and benevolence of the gardener they were apprenticed to. This garden boy is pictured in *c.* 1910.

departments of the garden, and adding management of staff to his repertoire of skills. Depending on the size and complexity of the garden, a foreman might progress to become a general foreman or deputy head gardener before being ready to apply for a position as head gardener.

The head gardener of a large garden had to show talents beyond his horticultural skills. He would be expected to manage a large team of gardeners and oversee the work of all the garden departments, ensuring that seasonal tasks were done at appropriate times and that all work met the exacting standards required. He had to satisfy the requirements of the owner of the garden, often liaising with the lady of the house on colour schemes and planting plans, and was subject to the family's whims and impulses. He was responsible for a large budget and would have to keep tight control of spending on wages and garden sundries, keeping his accounts in order for regular inspection by his employer's accountant or estate manager.

The head gardener was also required to be a man of taste, with a certain level of artistic ability. The layout of a garden was often conceived by an architect or designer brought in by the garden owner, but the head gardener could also be called upon to create a garden to realise the ideas of his employer. Some head gardeners were given more artistic freedom than others, depending on the nature of their employer. A garden owner with an interest in botany might encourage the introduction of new plants from abroad into the garden, creating an arboretum or an alpine collection, and allowing the head gardener to show off his horticultural skills. The annual display of summer bedding provided the ideal opportunity for a head gardener to showcase his artistic talents as each year a new colour scheme or pattern could be devised.

A head gardener of a smaller establishment might be working single-handed, or with one or two gardeners with whom to share the workload. In the newly created suburbs, the professional classes were making gardens and employing head gardeners to manage them, but they might also take an active interest in horticulture themselves, thus limiting the responsibilities of

Left: A nineteenth-century bedding plan from Stagenhoe in Hertfordshire indicates the level of artistry required by a head gardener when designing annual bedding displays.

Overleaf: Three young apprentices are pictured alongside the experienced gardeners from whom they will learn their trade.

A large kitchen garden would have a range of glasshouses, divided into sections for the cultivation of different fruits. An illustration of a peach house from 1879 shows how the fruit could be trained up frames to maximise yield.

Fig. 47.—Weeks's Peach House.

the head gardener. At a large and renowned establishment, the head gardener would not expect to carry out any practical work himself. He would know exactly what was happening in the garden through regular inspections and by overseeing the work of his foremen, and he might engage in specialised technical work such as hybridisation or propagating orchids or ferns, depending on his particular interests.

A large garden was divided into various departments, each with its own foreman in charge, and a trainee gardener would have to work in each department to gain experience in different forms of garden craft. The formal gardens and shrubberies had to be maintained in perfect condition for garden walks and views from the windows of the house, with bedding planted and lawns mown. The kitchen garden provided all the produce needed for the family, both while at home and also when staying at their other residences, where it was transported to arrive in peak condition for presentation at table. Gardeners working in the kitchen garden would be responsible for growing fruit and vegetables for consumption all year round, and so, as well as the walled garden where hardy fruit would be trained up the walls and vegetables cultivated in neatly sectioned beds, much was grown in glasshouses. There were ranges for peaches, grapes, melons and cucumbers and a specialised pit for pineapples.

There was a hierarchy in place between departments, with some requiring more horticultural expertise or practical skill than others. A foreman in the kitchen garden might seek career advancement to become foreman of the

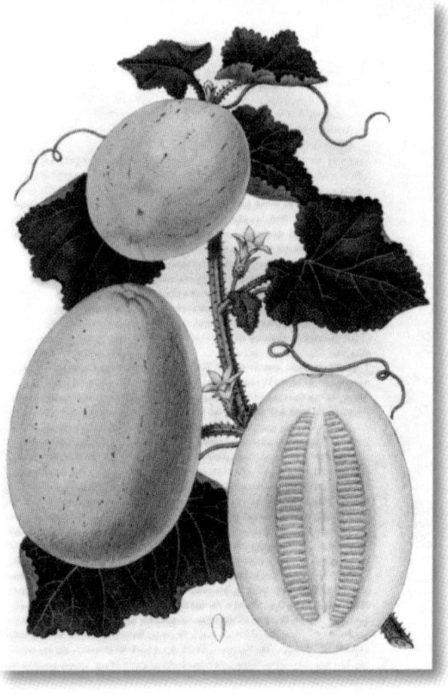

Top left: The new species of orchids being introduced from abroad prompted a mania of collecting with their exotic forms and colours, shown in an illustration from *Belgique Horticole* from 1851–4.

Top right: Grapes were raised in a vine house, the fruit being forced to provide an out-of-season delicacy.

Bottom left: Peaches were a favourite Victorian glasshouse fruit, ideal for displaying on the dining table.

Bottom right: Melons were grown in glasshouses using special net bags to support their weight on the vine.

flower garden, and then progress to working in the conservatory, with the forcing department deemed the most prestigious in terms of skill and status. The forcing of fruit and vegetables to provide out-of-season delicacies was considered an essential part of life in the Victorian country house and was a topic of much one-upmanship between both gardeners and owners. To serve an out-of-season strawberry or a home-grown pineapple, or to decorate the

Floral decorations for the dining table were at their most elaborate from the 1870s to the end of the nineteenth century. Multi-tiered flower stands, like the one shown here, were used by head gardeners, who were responsible for arranging the flowers as well as growing them.

table at Christmas with a bouquet of flowers from the glasshouse, was a display of wealth and prestige, demonstrating not only the skill of the head gardener, but also the superiority of his employer.

Florist's flowers were also grown in the garden to provide cut flowers for the house, and their cultivation was a further specialist garden department. Flowers were grown either in a cutting garden – or 'reserve garden' – or in borders flanking the central path through the kitchen garden, providing a decorative screen to the rows of vegetables. When the family were spending the season at their London home, cut flowers were transported daily from their country estate, arriving on the overnight train. After cutting the flowers, gardeners would carefully wrap them in spinach leaves for protection and then pack them in cases filled with sphagnum moss. Each bunch would be labelled with instructions for the house staff detailing which vase to use and which room the arrangement was intended for.

The head gardener would be obliged to keep up with the latest fashions in floral arrangements and acquire the necessary skills to master the delicate art of floristry. The ladies of the house generally arranged the flowers for the bedrooms, but the head gardener was responsible for the main reception rooms. In the winter months, when cut flowers from the garden were scarce, foliage plants and exotics from the glasshouse were brought into the house and arranged in pots, being swiftly replaced with a pristine specimen the moment they were past their prime. For special occasions, the head gardener would not only have to create splendid floral arrangements to decorate the reception rooms and dining table, but would also be expected to supply fresh flowers to adorn the dresses and hair of the ladies, always fulfilling their exacting requirements as to colour, size and fragrance.

The demand for elaborate floral decorations in the late nineteenth century was such that floristry became a specialist branch of the gardening profession. Books and articles were

Foliage plants, such as the palms in this advertisement from 1895, were popular in Victorian drawing rooms. The head gardener had to keep a close eye on houseplants and replace them before they passed their prime.

published on the subject, and specialised floristry products and flower stands were marketed. Some talented gardeners set up in business offering their services in floral design, and others with an aptitude for propagation established nursery businesses to supply the growing demand for plants.

Above: By the mid-nineteenth century floral art had become a specialism of the gardening trade, with businesses established to meet the increasing demand for floral decorations.

Right: Publications such as *The Floricultural Cabinet and Florist's Magazine*, shown here in an edition from 1840, enabled gardeners to keep up with fashions in floral decoration.

Opposite, top: A cutting from *Gardeners Illustrated* shows two advertisements placed in 1884: one by a gardener seeking work, the other by an employer in search of a gardener.

Gardeners on private estates were often appointed by recommendation from their previous employer, so ambitious gardeners were keen to make a good impression and to work under head gardeners who commanded some influence in the profession. By the 1860s, advertisements began to appear in the horticultural press, both from garden owners with situations vacant and from gardeners advertising their services to potential employers. Gardening magazines and journals proliferated in the mid-nineteenth century and were read by both garden owners and professional gardeners, thus providing an ideal forum for recruitment.

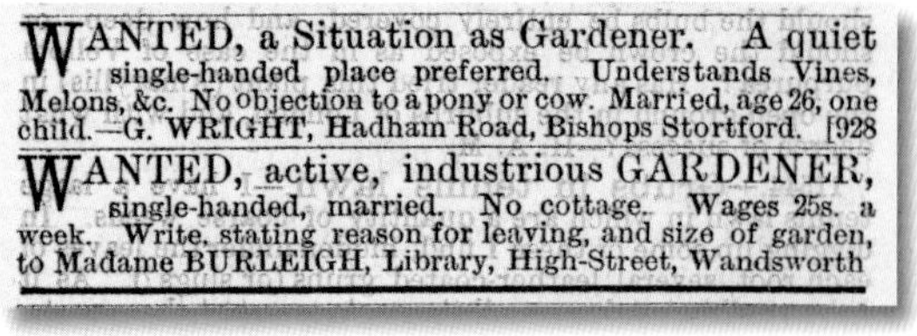
WANTED, a Situation as Gardener. A quiet single-handed place preferred. Understands Vines, Melons, &c. No objection to a pony or cow. Married, age 26, one child.—G. WRIGHT, Hadham Road, Bishops Stortford. [928

WANTED, active, industrious GARDENER, single-handed, married. No cottage. Wages 25s. a week. Write, stating reason for leaving, and size of garden, to Madame BURLEIGH, Library, High-Street, Wandsworth

Not all gardeners were employed in private service: some worked in nurseries, and others grew fruit and vegetables in market gardens. Those who could not afford the necessary training, or were unwilling or unable to travel to other parts of the country to find employment, advertised their services as jobbing gardeners, taking work where they could find it. Such work was often poorly paid and seasonal, offering little opportunity for advancement. Women were often employed as casual labourers

Men and women with varying levels of horticultural skills were employed in market gardens, established in or near towns and cities to provide a plentiful supply of fruit and vegetables for market.

doing weeding and other menial work, and seasonal garden jobs such as grass-cutting were done by hired labourers. Before the invention of the lawnmower, grass was cut by teams of labourers using scythes. This task was done in the early morning when the grass was still wet with dew. Because of the antisocial hours, the low pay and the physically demanding and repetitive nature of the work, such labourers commanded little respect and were barely regarded as gardeners at all.

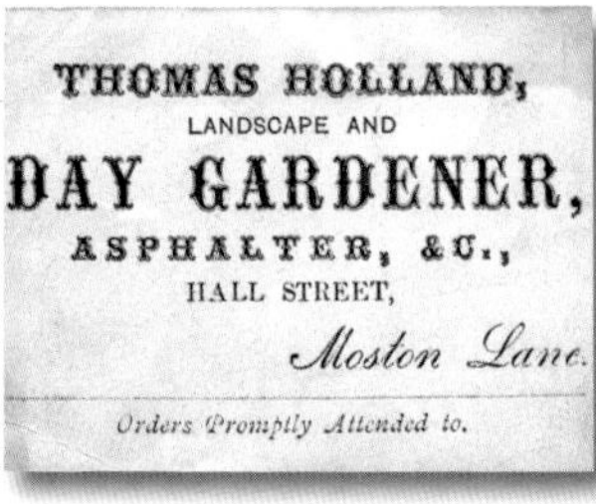

Jobbing gardeners had to find enough work to support themselves financially, advertising their services locally and distributing trade cards.

Below: A wage bill from 1863 details payments to a team of labourers for barrowing manure. The lowest paid was given just a shilling a day, and five of the six labourers were women.

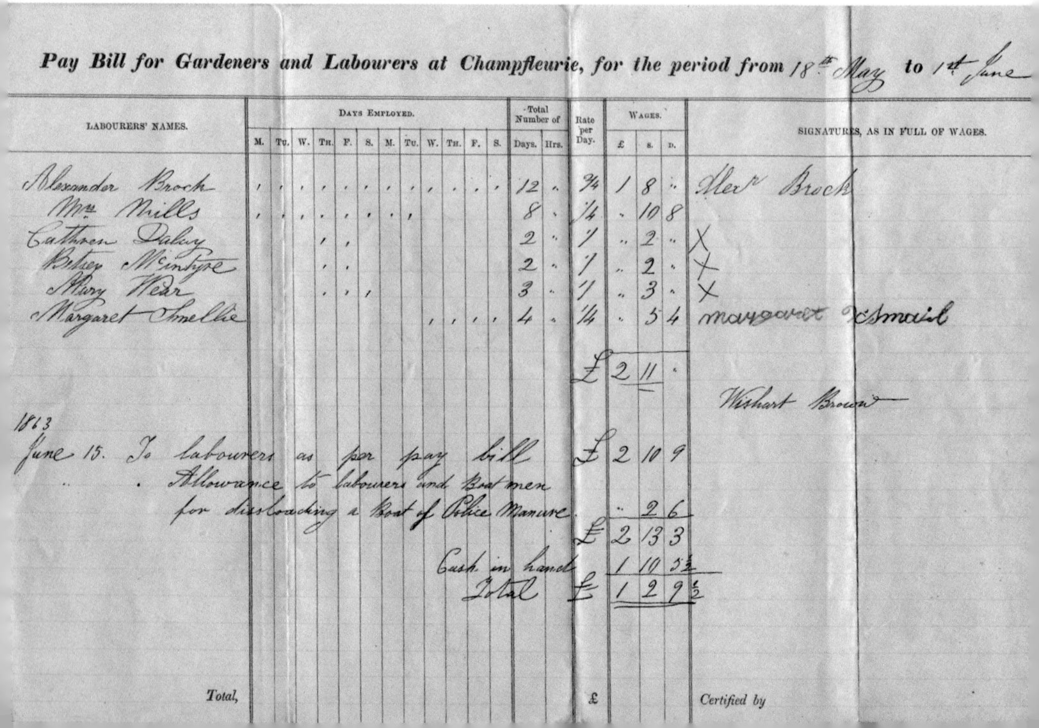

Pay Bill for Gardeners and Labourers at Champfleurie, for the period from 18th May **to** 1st June

LABOURERS' NAMES.	DAYS EMPLOYED. M.	TU.	W.	TH.	F.	S.	M.	TU.	W.	TH.	F.	S.	Total Number of Days.	Hrs.	Rate per Day.	WAGES. £	s.	D.	SIGNATURES, AS IN FULL OF WAGES.
Alexander Brock	'	'	'	'	'	'	'	'	'	'	'	'	12	..	2/4	1	8	..	Alexr Brock
Mrs Mills	'	'	'	'	'	'	'	'					8	.	1/4	.	10	8	
Cathren Daley				'	'								2	..	1/	..	2	..	X
Betsey McIntyre				'	'								2	..	1/	..	2	.	X
Mary Wear				'	'	'							3	..	1/	..	3	.	X
Margaret Smellie									'	'	'	'	4	.	1/4	.	5	4	margaret Smail
															£	2	11	.	
																			Wishart Brown

1863
June 15. To labourers as per pay bill £ 2 10 9
" . Allowance to labourers and Boat men for disloading a Boat of Police Manure .. 2 6
£ 2 13 3
Cash in hand 1 10 5½
Total £ 1 2 9½

Total, £ Certified by

TRAINING AND APPRENTICESHIPS

A CAREER in gardening accorded with the Victorian ideal of improvement, resulting in moral and intellectual advancement, as well as teaching practical skills. To succeed in the profession, a young man would need determination and dedication, be willing to work hard for long hours, and have the motivation and discipline to spend his evenings engaged in personal study. He would need to be a quick learner, willing to take instruction from his superiors, taking pride in his work, and striving for advancement. Many garden boys were the sons of gardeners or agricultural workers, following in their fathers' footsteps in the cultivation and tending of plants, and accustomed to working with nature.

Before undertaking an apprenticeship, a candidate would need to have a good basic education, being schooled in reading, writing and arithmetic, and ideally with a working knowledge of geometry and Latin. Intellectual ability would need to be matched by physical strength as trainees faced the arduous and demanding tasks of barrowing manure, stoking boilers, raking leaves and digging.

To secure a position as an apprentice, a charge would be paid to the head gardener of the establishment, known as the 'apprentice fee'. This would either be paid in advance or be deducted from weekly wages, and the system was open to abuse by unscrupulous head gardeners, who were at liberty to charge as much as they liked and to pocket the money for themselves. As there was no standardised training programme, the quality of apprenticeships varied greatly, and progress was dependent on the determination of the apprentice and the benevolence of the head gardener.

A good head gardener would give his apprentice a grounding in all aspects of garden work, allowing him to learn skills and techniques from the foremen of the various garden departments. This passing-on of practical experience built up by generations of gardeners was supplemented by

A young gardener was expected to study horticultural books and journals to supplement his practical training. Many books were published in the nineteenth century as printing was mechanised, the tax on paper was abolished, and people became more literate.

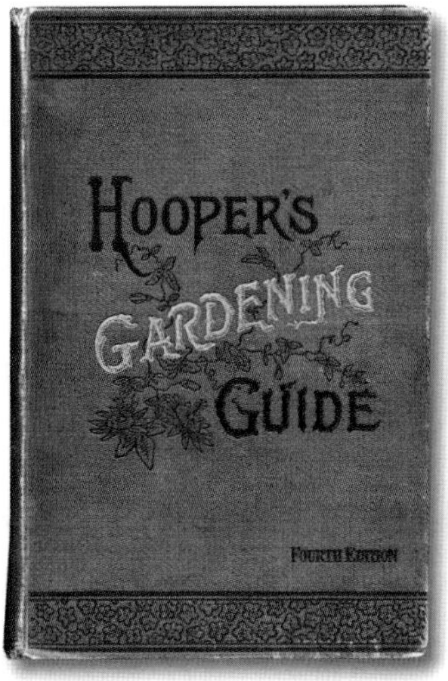

John Loudon was a trained gardener who campaigned to raise the status of the horticultural profession. He wrote books and articles and founded *The Gardener's Magazine* in 1826.

study of the theory of horticulture, with the combination of principle and practice resulting in a well-rounded education. The apprentice was encouraged to keep a daily journal in which to record garden tasks, horticultural techniques and botanical notes, and the head gardener would determine when the trainee had attained the requisite amount of skills and knowledge to move on to the next stage of his career and apply for a position as a journeyman gardener.

John Loudon (1783–1843), the great horticultural champion of the early nineteenth century, claimed that 'a gardener can no more acquire his profession without books than he can without tools'. Personal study was integral to the training of a young gardener, who was expected to understand, in addition to horticultural practice, the principles of botany, plant physiology, geometry, geology, meteorology, chemistry, natural history, surveying, architectural drawing, grammar, book-keeping and foreign languages.

In this photograph from c. 1905 an aged gardener is shown instructing a garden boy in cultivation techniques in the kitchen garden, passing on years of horticultural experience to the next generation.

Fortunately for the aspiring gardener, Loudon had assembled all the requisite knowledge in his *Encyclopaedia of Gardening*, first published in 1822. The encyclopaedia was read by gardeners and garden owners alike and commanded great professional respect, going through six editions in Loudon's lifetime, its popularity serving as proof of the demand for high-quality, accessible horticultural information. Loudon campaigned for the rights of working gardeners throughout his career, culminating in the posthumous publication in 1845 of his book *Self-instruction for Young Gardeners*, which covers all the subjects necessary for a career in gardening in 240 closely printed pages.

Advances in printing technology and the abolition of the tax on paper in 1861 made newspapers, books and magazines more popular with the increasingly literate and self-improving Victorians, and the growing interest in horticulture prompted the publication of a number of gardening books and journals. There were manuals to be consulted on the cultivation of plants from ferns to roses, books aimed at the amateur gardener or the specialist collector, nursery catalogues and botanical monographs. There was also a proliferation of magazines aimed at professional gardeners, among them *The Gardener's Magazine*, founded by Loudon in 1826. Aside from providing a voice for Loudon's own opinions on horticultural matters, the monthly magazine offered book reviews, advice on cultivation, descriptions

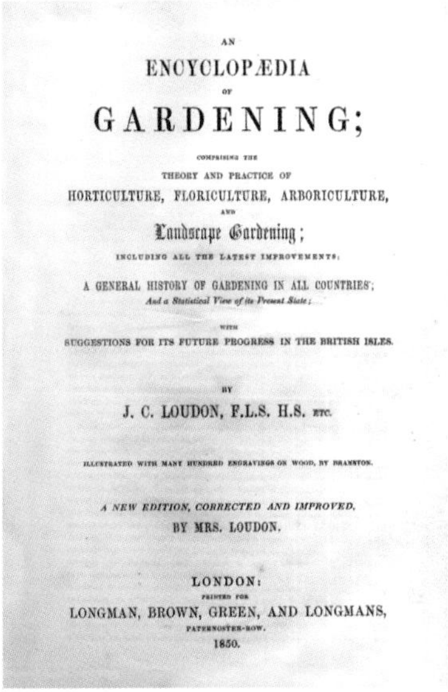

AN
ENCYCLOPÆDIA
OF
GARDENING;
COMPRISING THE
THEORY AND PRACTICE OF
HORTICULTURE, FLORICULTURE, ARBORICULTURE,
AND
Landscape Gardening;
INCLUDING ALL THE LATEST IMPROVEMENTS;
A GENERAL HISTORY OF GARDENING IN ALL COUNTRIES;
And a Statistical View of its Present State;
WITH
SUGGESTIONS FOR ITS FUTURE PROGRESS IN THE BRITISH ISLES.

BY
J. C. LOUDON, F.L.S. H.S. ETC.

ILLUSTRATED WITH MANY HUNDRED ENGRAVINGS ON WOOD, BY BRANSTON.

A NEW EDITION, CORRECTED AND IMPROVED,
BY MRS. LOUDON.

LONDON:
PRINTED FOR
LONGMAN, BROWN, GREEN, AND LONGMANS,
PATERNOSTER-ROW.
1850.

Loudon's book *An Encyclopaedia of Gardening* was published in 1822 and was reprinted into the 1870s, being regarded as the standard text on horticulture.

Horticultural magazines advertised the many new gardening products and services available, as can be seen in these pages from *The Garden Oracle* of 1895.

of newly introduced plants, articles on gardens visited by correspondents, advertisements for products and services, and a forum for gardening debate. In 1841 *The Gardener's Chronicle* was launched as a weekly publication, founded by the eminent head gardener Joseph Paxton, and became the most influential horticultural periodical of the era.

Campaigners such as Loudon recognised the discrepancy between the price of the books and magazines necessary for self-improvement and the level of gardeners' wages. The most willing and ambitious gardeners would be impeded in their advancement if they did not have access to the necessary resources. With this in mind, Loudon introduced the concept of Gardeners' Improvement Societies, operated on the model used by other professions. A subscription was paid by members, who then enjoyed the benefits of access to books and journals, attendance at lectures, and the opportunity to share the company of other gardeners in what could be a lonely profession. Members were also encouraged to present papers on topics of interest,

The popularity of gardening prompted the invention of labour-saving gadgets, such as these multi-bladed shears advertised in *Gardening Illustrated* in 1879.

sharing horticultural expertise and technical advancements with their peers. In large gardens where many gardeners were employed, improvement societies were founded and became a useful part of an apprentice's training. However, the gardener apprenticed at a smaller establishment in a remote country location was necessarily isolated from other members of his profession,

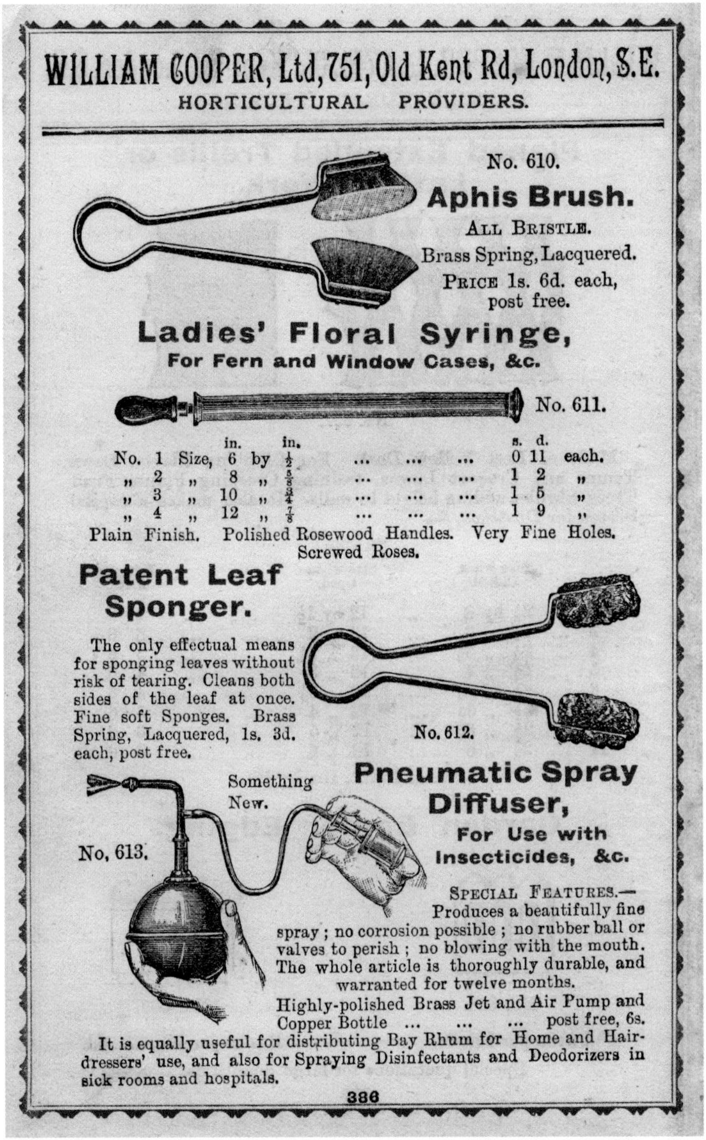

Companies specialising in the supply of horticultural equipment were established in the nineteenth century, selling all manner of gadgets to an enthusiastic gardening public.

and reliant on the qualities of the head gardener to progress in his training, together with whatever resources of his own he could muster. Although public libraries were being established from the late 1850s, they depended largely on philanthropy and were located in urban areas inaccessible to many working gardeners.

Gardening periodicals also served to keep gardeners up to date with the advancements in science and technology that were having such a profound effect on their profession. New inventions, such as the lawnmower, were changing the way gardeners worked, and numerous other labour-saving machines and gadgets were designed, with varying levels of success. Weeding machines, hosepipes, sunshades, fumigators and cucumber straighteners flooded the market as ingenious Victorians tried to find a solution to every horticultural problem, with pragmatic gardeners giving their opinion on their merits, or otherwise, in the gardening press.

These gardeners, photographed in 1909, demonstrate the use of early lawnmowers that were pushed by one gardener and pulled by another to achieve the best results.

As plant hunters scoured the globe for new species, gardeners had to keep up with the new plant introductions and their particular methods of cultivation. In 1500 there were about two hundred plants in cultivation in Britain, yet by 1840 there were over eighteen thousand. These new plants brought prestige to the gardening profession, and ambitious head gardeners vied with one another to be the first to raise a new species from seed or to bring a plant to flower for the first time under their nurturing care. Some gardeners and nurserymen experimented with hybridisation, producing new cultivars suited to the British climate, with the desired vigour, size and colour to meet Victorian tastes. In a fast-changing world, gardening magazines allowed professionals to voice their opinions and exchange ideas with other gardeners, offering the opportunity to ambitious gardeners to make a name for themselves in the profession.

The most ambitious and talented young gardeners could apply to work and train at the garden of the Horticultural Society. The Horticultural Society was founded in 1804, with the instruction of young gardeners being one of its original aims. In 1823 the society established an experimental garden at Chiswick where young men were employed as under-gardeners and trained in the horticultural practices of each department. Applicants, who had to be unmarried and between eighteen and twenty-six years of age, were expected to have some experience of gardening, together with a good basic education. When the training was complete, the officers of the society would recommend their trainees for suitable positions in private gardens, thus giving them a prominent start to their career.

Similar horticultural training was offered at the Royal Botanic Society's garden at Regent's Park from the 1840s, at the Royal Botanic Gardens, Kew, from 1859, and at the Royal Botanic Gardens in Edinburgh from 1892, but there was no standardised curriculum of study or classification of achievement. In an attempt to address this deficiency, in 1866 the

Dahlias were introduced to Britain in the early years of the nineteenth century and were extensively hybridised. By 1840 Victorian gardeners had over five hundred different cultivars to choose from.

first examinations for gardeners were introduced, administered by the Royal Society of Arts. Candidates could sit three-hour examinations to gain diplomas in botany, floriculture, fruit and vegetable culture, book-keeping, mensuration and practical geometry. The next tier of examinations was set by what was now the Royal Horticultural Society (it having been granted a royal charter by Prince Albert in 1861) and led to the award of Associate of the Royal Horticultural Society, with first- and second-class divisions. Despite the incentive of reimbursement of travel expenses and cash prizes offered by *The Gardener's Chronicle* to high-scoring candidates, interest from the profession was lacklustre. Employers did not recognise the qualification, and the award of a certificate did not bring an increase in wages or guarantee career advancement.

By 1893 the exams had been standardised by the Royal Horticultural Society to become the General Examination, in which candidates had to pass two written papers at the society's London headquarters in Vincent Square before their practical knowledge was tested over two days in the new garden at Wisley. Students were prepared for the examinations at many of the horticultural institutions established around the country at the end of the nineteenth century. In 1889 Swanley College in Kent admitted its first horticultural students and

One of the most prestigious places for a young gardener to train was at the Royal Botanic Gardens, Kew. These gardeners are pictured working in the American Gardens at Kew in 1906.

was to gain a notable reputation in the gardening profession. The curriculum covered chemistry, zoology, meteorology and botany, and students had to achieve a first-class pass in the Royal Horticultural Society examinations in order to be awarded their Swanley Certificate.

Some courses covered more than practical horticulture and botanical science, preparing young gardeners for the realities of working on a private estate or running their own market garden or nursery business. The Crystal Palace School of Gardening, established in 1881 with Edward Milner as principal, offered an eighteen-month course teaching students how to master book-keeping, order sundries from suppliers and manage garden staff, in addition to practical training in horticulture and hard landscaping. Writtle College in Essex was established as an agricultural training institution in 1893 and opened a School of Horticulture in 1896, following the appointment of Charles Wakely as the first horticultural instructor, and the School of Agriculture and Horticulture in Uckfield, East Sussex, was established in the early 1890s. For a fee, schools such as these offered horticultural training that could supplement the experience gained through an apprenticeship and, on completion of the course, students were recommended for suitable gardening positions.

A group of students taking instruction in practical horticulture at Writtle College in Essex, photographed in 1901.

WORKING CONDITIONS

THE STATUS of gardening as a profession rose in the course of the nineteenth century to become a respectable career, with young gardeners working their way up from garden boy to foreman or head gardener, and enjoying the social status that came with positions of management. The route to the top was long and hard, however, and only the most dedicated, motivated and capable gardeners would fulfil their ambitions.

John Loudon, through his many publications, sought to champion the rights of working gardeners and to raise gardening to the level of other learned professions in the estimation of society. Loudon himself had trained as a gardener, being apprenticed to a nurseryman in his native Scotland, while also attending classes in agriculture, botany and chemistry at Edinburgh University, and so he was well aware of the mental and physical privations faced when embarking upon a career in gardening.

Loudon campaigned for better wages and conditions for working gardeners, but believed that young gardeners had to earn the respect that their profession craved. In his *Encyclopaedia of Gardening* he urged young men entering the profession to behave with decorum, present themselves neatly and defer to their employer: 'Remember, you are paid and maintained by and for the use and pleasure of your employer, who may no more wish to see a dirty, ragged, uncouth-looking, grinning or conceited biped in his garden, than a starved, haggard, untutored horse in his stable.' In return for the respect and hard work of their gardeners, Loudon believed that employers had a duty to improve the working conditions and prospects of their employees, and encouraged estate owners to provide gardening books and a quiet place for private study, as well as decent accommodation and wages.

The wages of a gardener working on a private estate were lower than those of a domestic servant, and also lower than those paid in other trades such as carpentry or printing. Despite years of training and personal study, gardeners were paid a third of the wage paid to a bricklayer, who was likely to be illiterate. Campaigners such as Loudon argued that not only was it hard to live on such a low wage, but that without more money it was impossible

Opposite: A group of market gardeners takes a break among the fields of cabbages and potatoes, photographed c. 1900.

An employer would expect his gardeners to look smart and behave respectfully, and fines were levied in many gardens for untidiness and negligence. This neatly dressed garden boy was photographed in *c.* 1910.

for a gardener to improve his social status and thus gain the respect his profession deserved.

Gardeners' wages rose steadily throughout the nineteenth century, but there remained a marked disparity when compared with other trades. In 1860 an apprentice was paid from 3s to 4s a week, and a journeyman from 10s to 14s. By 1880 the wages of a journeyman had risen to 12s to 18s a week, while men working in other craft professions such as blacksmithing and weaving were still paid significantly more, their weekly wage ranging from 25s to 30s.

Being employed as a gardener brought certain perks that compensated to some extent for the low wages. Whereas other tradesmen were required to provide and maintain a set of tools at their own expense, gardeners found all they needed neatly stored in the tool shed. Apprentice gardeners and journeymen were also usually provided with basic accommodation, and many employers also supplied vegetables from the kitchen garden and coal or logs in winter. The quality of the accommodation available varied greatly from garden to garden but usually comprised a garden bothy located near the kitchen garden and shared by all the junior gardeners.

The best of these bothies had beds arranged in dormitory accommodation and washing facilities, with tables, chairs and candles provided for evening study. A woman was employed to wash the gardeners' clothes, cook basic meals and keep the bothy clean. From contemporary accounts, it appears that some employers showed little concern for the welfare of their lower garden staff, with conditions in some bothies ranging from unpleasant to downright unhealthy.

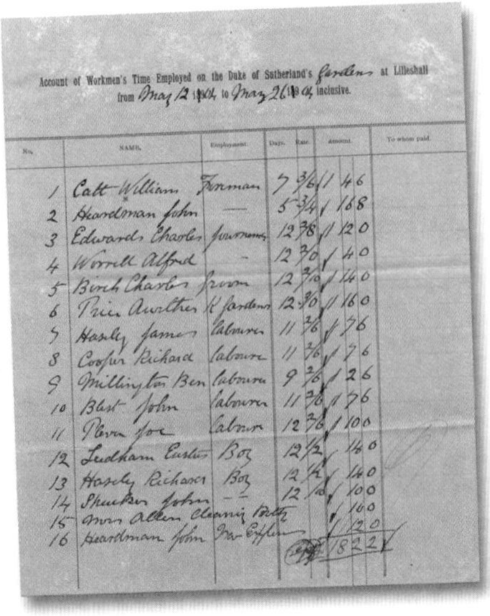

Account of Workmen's Time Employed on the Duke of Sutherland's Gardens at Lilleshall from May 12 1904 to May 26 1904 inclusive.

No.	Name.	Employment.	Days.	Rate.	Amount.	To whom paid.
1	Catt William	Foreman	7	3/6	1 4 6	
2	Heardman John	—	5	3/4	16 8	
3	Edwards Charles	Journeyman	12	2/8	1 12 0	
4	Worrell Alfred	–	12	2/0	1 4 0	
5	Birch Charles	Groom	12	2/10	1 14 0	
6	Price Awlther	K gardener	12	3/0	1 16 0	
7	Hasley James	labourer	11	2/6	1 7 6	
8	Cooper Richard	labourer	11	2/6	1 7 6	
9	Millington Ben	labourer	9	2/6	1 2 6	
10	Blest John	labourer	11	2/6	1 7 6	
11	Plevin Joe	labourer	12	2/6	1 10 0	
12	Ludham Euston	Boy	12	1/2	14 0	
13	Hasley Richard	Boy	12	1/2	14 0	
14	Shucker John	– –	12	10	10 0	
15	Mrs Allen	Cleaning Bothy			16 0	
16	Heardman John	Mr Effler			1 12 0	
					18 2 2	

A wage bill from the gardens at Lilleshall in Shropshire from 1904 shows that the highest daily rates were paid to the foreman and kitchen gardener, and the lowest paid received just 10d a day. A payment was made to a woman for cleaning the garden bothy.

An illustration from the *Gardener's Almanac* of 1843 shows a selection of tools used by gardeners, which were provided at their place of work.

Manufacturing processes were improved in the nineteenth century, but the design of garden tools has remained the same for centuries.

Accommodation was described as cold, damp and gloomy, and young gardeners returning from a hard day of physical work had to hunker down on a bed made of planks set on an earth floor. An open fire without a grate provided some welcome heat but cracks under the doors and gaps in the ceiling resulted in drafts that countered any comfort. When the weather was wet, the occupants had to avoid leaky roofs and damp walls and dry their clothes as best they could. Tables and chairs, when provided at all, were in the form of tree stumps and bare planks.

Where no woman was employed to cook for the 'bothy boys', they had to provide their own meals, often consisting of little more than milk and oatmeal. The gardeners were required to supply their own bowls and spoons, and also their own bedding, with the sheets being seldom washed. Such poor conditions would hardly encourage the young gardener to linger in the bothy to study horticultural books, and it is no

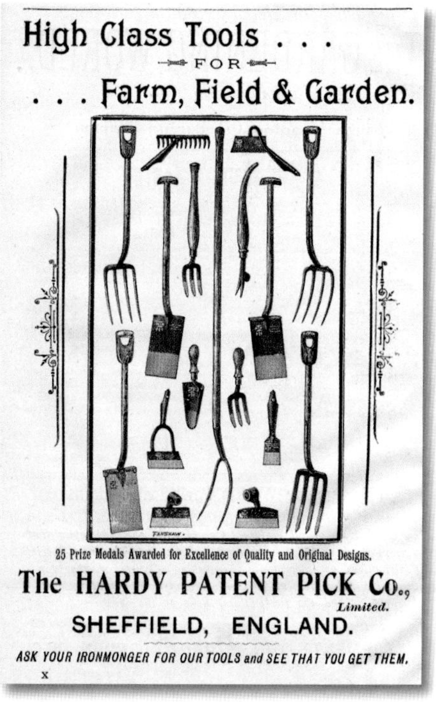

The head gardener's house at Levens Hall in Cumbria, pictured in 1906, is conveniently situated on the edge of the topiary gardens.

The garden bothy at Kelmarsh Hall in Northamptonshire was built back-to-back with the glasshouse range in the kitchen garden, accommodating the young gardeners close to their place of work and away from the domestic staff.

surprise that many were tempted to escape these domestic privations for the relative comfort of the local alehouse.

On a large estate, a house would be provided for the head gardener and his family, as by this stage in his career he was permitted to marry. A supportive and conscientious wife could be an asset to a head gardener as she could help with administrative tasks such as accounts and wages. The head gardener's accommodation, like that of the junior garden staff, was usually situated close to the kitchen garden and its offices, which served

The architectural grandeur of the house provided for the head gardener at Stagenhoe in Hertfordshire reflects his prominent position in the household.

At Sandringham in Norfolk the head gardener's house provides an attractive architectural backdrop to the bedding displays.

to keep the head gardener near his place of work, and also away from the domestic staff, who would be lodged in separate male and female accommodation within the main house. The indoor and outdoor staff met only through professional necessity, with the lower ranks having no occasion ever to encounter one another.

The working day in the Victorian era was a demanding twelve-hour shift for most employees, and it was no different for gardeners. They were expected to work from six o'clock in the morning, when the first job of the day was to unlock the garden gates, to six o'clock in the evening, with an hour for breakfast and an hour for dinner. Holidays amounted to three feast days a year. A gardener's daily jobs would vary from season to season, and summer work could include grass-cutting using a scythe, which would

Before the invention of the lawnmower, grass was cut with a scythe. In large gardens, seasonal labourers were often hired to carry out this work, which was arduous, repetitive and physically demanding.

commence at four o'clock in the morning while the grass was still wet with dew and easier to cut. The working week ran from Monday to Saturday, but duties such as watering plants and stoking the glasshouse boilers had to be carried out on Sundays as on any other day, and this extra work often went unpaid.

The junior garden staff were obliged to carry out the jobs that required the most antisocial hours, and the garden boy often had to sleep next to the boiler to ensure it was always sufficiently stoked and supplied with coal. It was imperative that the temperature in the glasshouses was maintained to the exact levels set by the head gardener, which would vary from glasshouse to glasshouse depending on the plants cultivated within. In warm weather vents would have to be opened, and in cold weather the fires stoked, operations that required twenty-four hour vigilance with no margin for error. Fines were levied by the head gardener on employees who made costly mistakes, and also for poor conduct in the garden. Negligence, such as forgetting to water plants or not ventilating glasshouses correctly, was a punishable offence, and fines were imposed for swearing, smoking, reporting late for work and entering a glasshouse with dirty boots.

Much of the work of the lower garden staff was repetitive and laborious. To create the annual bedding displays, gardeners had to propagate and pot on thousands of plants each year.

If treated well, gardeners were loyal to the garden owners who employed them. Unlike urban factory workers with their faceless industrialist managers, gardeners would see their employers regularly and were part of an extended family of domestic staff. They might grumble about their pay and conditions, but rarely would they band together against their employer, and the isolated nature of gardening meant that attempts to form workers' unions had little success.

The Order of Free Gardeners was a friendly society set up to allow workers to save for their retirement and provide insurance in times of infirmity.

Such loyalty also required a gardener to be tolerant of his employer's impulses and ideas, and to express patience with the whims of family members and guests. If the bedding was trampled on by playful children or the peaches were picked from the glasshouse, the gardeners had to repair the damage without complaint. As an employee, a gardener had to act according to the wishes of his employer, whether or not they accorded with his own artistic tastes and horticultural expertise. The gardener was a servant, obliged to stand aside and allow his employer to take the credit for his efforts, sacrificing his triumphs to the glory of the garden. Prizes at horticultural shows were awarded in the name of the wealthy owner, rather than the talented gardener who, using his horticultural skills and experience, had nurtured the plants into prize-winning specimens.

Many gardeners worked into old age, with retirement coming only when they were physically incapable of further work. Loyal staff on large estates were often allowed to remain in their houses on retirement, but many gardeners were not so fortunate. In 1839 the Benevolent Institution for the Relief of Aged and Indigent Gardeners and Their Widows was founded to provide pensions for gardeners in need, with money raised through voluntary contributions and an annual fundraising dinner.

Friendly societies proliferated in the nineteenth century, when the only welfare provided by the state was the workhouse. Members paid a small regular payment that provided insurance in times of sickness and a pension on retirement. The Order of Free Gardeners was established in Scotland in the seventeenth century by working gardeners to promote their profession and to provide financial assistance to members in need. The members initially consisted of working gardeners and garden owners but in later years members were accepted from other professions. The Order of Free Gardeners developed alongside the Freemasons and adopted some of their trappings and symbolism, with the gardener's knife added to the Freemasons' emblem of compass and square to represent the pruning of vice and the propagation of virtue. By the end of the nineteenth century there were over ten thousand members of the Order of Free Gardeners in the Lothians of Scotland, and the society had crossed the border, with branches being established throughout England. Through friendly societies, gardeners were able to provide for their future and avoid destitution in times of illness, injury or infirmity.

The Free Gardeners adopted much of the ritual and symbolism of the Freemasons. This apron depicts the gardener's knife above the mason's compass and square, while the letters P, G, H and E represent the initials of the four rivers of the Garden of Eden.

WOMEN GARDENERS

To victorian sensibilities, gardening was an eminently suitable occupation for a lady, combining fresh air and moderate exercise with self-improvement. Middle-class women took up gardening as a hobby, tending their own suburban patch, and developing interests in the associated activities of flower-arranging, fern-collecting and botanical art. Tools were manufactured specifically for female use, and gardening manuals for ladies were published, giving instruction in garden tasks suitable for women, and advice on planting and colour schemes. John Loudon's wife, Jane, exceeded the sales of her husband's horticultural books with her own successful volumes aimed at women gardeners, such as *Instructions in Gardening for Ladies* of 1840 and *The Ladies' Companion to the Flower Garden*, published in 1841. Herself a self-taught gardener, Jane Loudon recognised the need for simple, easy-to-follow gardening manuals aimed at the amateur gardener who was literate and enthusiastic but had little scientific knowledge or practical training.

Although gardening was acceptable as a hobby for women, as a profession it was regarded as unseemly. The garden bothy was a strictly male domain, so a traditional garden apprenticeship was out of the question, and women were deemed incapable of the heavy work involved in gardening. It was not until the last decade of the nineteenth century that women were offered places on horticultural training courses, and even then it was considered an unorthodox career path. Improvements in access to education and the rise of the professional middle classes created a group of young, educated, affluent women in search of an occupation acceptable to their place in society. Their options were limited to the respectable professions of teaching, nursing or working in a shop or office.

By the end of the nineteenth century, women had gained some rights that were paving the way towards equality. Social attitudes towards women were slowly changing, but they were still regarded primarily in their domestic role as wives and mothers. Manual work such as gardening was considered unsuitable for ladies until the advent of the First World War

Opposite: Photographed in 1903, Marie Studholme, a popular beauty of Victorian and Edwardian musical comedy, personifies the fashion for hobby gardening among refined ladies.

The popularity of gardening created a market for books specifically designed for amateur women gardeners, such as Louisa Johnson's *Every Lady Her Own Flower Gardener*, published in 1840.

forced a change in attitude. The jobs left behind by men departing for the trenches were taken up by women and provided an opportunity for them to prove their capability in professions such as gardening. The social change that followed in the aftermath of war eventually brought the vote to women and the freedom to pursue a career of their choosing.

It took time for women to be accepted in roles formerly dominated by men. Female gardeners were employed at the Royal Botanic

The collection and display of ferns was deemed a suitable occupation for ladies who had an interest in horticulture, and ornamental indoor fern cases brought gardening into the domestic realm.

Gardens, Kew, from 1896, with Annie Gulvin and Alice Hutchings being the first to take their place alongside male recruits, and they were soon joined by others. There was some initial consternation about what the female gardeners would wear, as skirts were liable to brush against the plants and damage them. The amusing novelty of women gardening in bloomers prompted ridicule in the press. In 1900 *Fun* magazine responded to this extraordinary sight in verse:

> They gardened in bloomers, the newspapers said;
> So to Kew without warning all Londoners sped:
> From the roofs of the buses they had a fine view
> Of the ladies in bloomers who gardened at Kew.

Botanical painting was a hobby that allowed women to pursue an interest in plants without breaking any of the social conventions associated with practical gardening. Some women had their work published, others displayed their paintings in albums.

Gardening was taught to schoolgirls for the value of its moral lessons. The feminine virtues of patience, diligence and tender care could be demonstrated through nurturing plants, and the girls would benefit from fresh air and exercise.

Three of the first women to be employed as gardeners at Kew were Alice Hutchings, Gertrude Cope and Eleanor Morland, who trained at Swanley College together. They are photographed wearing the same gardening uniform as their male colleagues, *c.* 1896.

To resolve the difficulty, the women were permitted to wear the same practical working clothes as their male colleagues, so they set to work in breeches, waistcoats, peaked caps and heavy boots, liberating them from the long skirts and tight waistbands of Victorian convention.

The women employed at Kew had received their horticultural training at Swanley College in Kent. The college was established in 1889 and began to admit female students in 1891. Women were housed in separate accommodation to the male students and were seated at the back of the classroom, always accompanied by a chaperone. The number of female students at the college increased, as did their success in examinations, and in 1901 the college became an all-female institution, with an excellent reputation for horticulture. Students were charged £80 a year for tuition, board and lodgings, and had to provide their own books, bedding, towels and dinner napkins. They also had to purchase their own uniform, which included a tunic and coat of Swanley tweed for winter and a lighter green tunic for summer, blouses, stockings, blazer, belt, jersey, brown felt or straw hat, strong brown boots, clogs, mackintosh, gardening gloves and a blue serge apron.

Two other graduates of Swanley College, Annie Morison and Lina Barker, moved north in 1897 to work at the Royal Botanic Garden in Edinburgh, where they were the first female gardeners to be employed. Recognising the need for horticultural training courses specifically for women, of which there were none in Scotland, they established the Edinburgh School of Gardening for Women in 1903, initially based at Inveresk but later moving to Corstorphine. Other gardening schools became established around this time, some specifically for women, and some, such as Writtle College in Essex, accepting women on a co-educational basis.

Practical training in agriculture and horticulture was made available to women through the initiative of Frances Evelyn Greville, Countess of Warwick (1861-1938). Known as 'Daisy', Lady Warwick was rich, hedonistic and independent, but also concerned with social justice. In order to provide employment opportunities for the daughters of professional families, she promoted the idea of working in rural occupations such as gardening and light farming, and in 1898 established the Lady Warwick Hostel in Reading. In association with Reading College, women were trained in horticulture, market gardening and fruit growing, as well as dairy work, poultry farming

Studley College was established in 1898 to train women in horticulture. The grounds at Studley Castle had ample space for glasshouses where the students could practise techniques of fruit production, as shown in this photograph of thegrape house, c. 1910.

and bee keeping. The college staff provided lessons on the theory of horticulture while practical work was done in the grounds of the hostel, under the management of the warden, Edith Bradley.

The courses proved popular and in 1899 two further hostels were opened in Reading, and in the first six years over two hundred students were enrolled. In 1903 the establishment moved to Studley Castle in Warwickshire, bought by Lady Warwick at her own expense for £25,000, and now named Lady Warwick College. The institution now operated independently of Reading College, offering its own classes and lectures. Lady Warwick's social causes and improvement schemes had soon expended most of her fortune and she was forced to scale back her activities, relinquishing control of the college in 1908. The school was renamed Studley College and by 1916 had been recognised by the Royal Horticultural Society as an approved training institution.

Another aristocratic lady concerned with training women for careers in horticulture was Frances, Viscountess Wolseley (1872–1936). Lady Wolseley was an ardent campaigner for agricultural reform, the revival of rural industries and fair pay for women, and when her family settled in rural Sussex she established the Glynde School for Lady Gardeners. Founded in 1902, the horticultural school offered two-year courses in gardening and garden design to young women in the grounds of her parents' house, moving to larger premises just outside Glynde village in 1907. The new site included student accommodation and a 5-acre teaching garden. The students were organised

Overleaf: Glynde School for Lady Gardeners was founded in 1902 by Frances Wolseley and provided horticultural training for women until the school closed in 1916.

The Cult

AN IDEAL VOCATION FOR LADIES

At the Glynde School: A lad

Gardening

ND WHERE IT CAN BE LEARNED

rimming the edges of the turf

The female students at Studley College learned through practical instruction in the college gardens. This photograph shows a lesson in pruning, *c.* 1910.

in military fashion, the working day beginning early, and the rules were rigidly enforced, with transgressions punished with fines, and good behaviour rewarded with medals. The students wore a uniform comprising a long skirt, white blouse and felt hat with a khaki-coloured coat, and for practical work, breeches, gaiters and boots. The breeches made gardening activities more manageable, but were worn under a short skirt to maintain respectability.

The school set high standards, both in horticulture and in the conduct of its students, and aimed to equip young women with the practical skills and artistic awareness essential for a career in gardening, although the focus on practical training was at the expense of science, with neither botany nor chemistry on the curriculum. Despite the patronage of influential figures such as Gertrude Jekyll, Ellen Willmott and William Robinson, the Royal Horticultural Society refused to recognise Glynde School as a training institution, and the students who sat official examinations rarely passed them.

Of those women who graduated from horticultural college, some took up teaching positions and others found employment at institutions such as the Royal Botanic Gardens, Kew, where they could continue their horticultural training while being paid a weekly wage. Annie Gulvin, one of the first women to work at Kew, was the first of them to be appointed head gardener in a private garden, aged only twenty. She was employed in the garden at Iscoed in Carmarthen, where she managed a staff of five and successfully improved the condition of the run-down garden and gained the respect of her fellow gardeners and employer. After a year, she moved on to Burstall in Suffolk but her horticultural career was to come to an end not long afterwards, prompted by her marriage in the summer of 1900. Her job at Burstall was taken on by her contemporary at Kew, Alice Hutchings, who had by then risen to the

A group of students at Glynde School, pictured in *c.* 1910. The women are wearing boots and breeches under their long gardening aprons.

position of sub-foreman of the alpine pits. Two years later she, too, was married and obliged to resign her post. The conventions of society, although slowly changing, still meant that it was socially unacceptable for married women of the middle classes to work. Women were forced to choose between a career and a family, and many of the early pioneers of horticultural training laid down their spades in favour of marriage.

The horticultural courses on offer to women were aimed at the middle classes. Fees were charged for lectures and practical tuition, and board and lodgings created further expense, as did the purchase of a uniform and stout boots. Gardening was becoming an accessible profession for middle-class women, while the working classes still provided female labour in private gardens and nurseries for the menial tasks of weeding, raking and picking, work that was poorly paid, physically demanding and seasonal.

Through the campaigning of women such as Lady Warwick and Lady Wolseley, the writings of Jane Loudon, and the determined contribution of working female gardeners, women were gradually gaining a place in the profession of horticulture. Reputations in garden design and plantsmanship were established by women such as Gertrude Jekyll, Norah Lindsay and Ellen Willmott as women made their mark in a male-dominated profession, and more and more women chose to enrol on horticultural courses to equip them for a career in gardening. During two world wars these skills proved vital as women filled the gardening positions of men who enlisted for war service, and it was women who fronted the campaign to 'Dig for Victory'.

As men departed for the front during the First World War, women took over their jobs at home, proving themselves to be capable of hard manual work such as gardening.

THE HEAD GARDENER

A SUCCESSFUL head gardener needed business acumen as well as horticultural talent. To ensure the smooth running of each department within the garden required an aptitude for staff management, with trusted foremen appointed to oversee the work of the junior gardeners. The garden finances had to be kept in good order, with sources of revenue, such as the sale of surplus garden produce, capitalised upon to balance the account books. The head gardener was responsible for the pleasure grounds, formal gardens, kitchen garden, cut flower garden, glasshouses, and floral decorations in the house, all of which had to be perfectly presented in all seasons. He had to predict and respond to the weather, ensure the health and vitality of the plants in his care and meet the exacting requirements of his employer.

While many tasks in the garden were routine and seasonal, carried out according to the weather and the calendar, some were more complex and required meticulous planning and organisation. The Victorian fashion for summer bedding required lengthy behind-the-scenes preparation to produce the stunning effects demanded by owners keen to make an impression. The design of the bedding was planned, often in consultation with the lady of the house for her guidance on colour scheme and layout, and the beds would be measured up, careful calculations being made to determine the number of plants required of each colour and species. The head gardener would then have to order the seeds and ensure there were adequate supplies of pots and compost available, as well as allocating space in the glasshouses for raising the seedlings. Depending on the size and complexity of the scheme, between ten thousand and fifty thousand plants might be required, and an experienced head gardener would put in place contingency plans to allow for unforeseen complications, such as pest infestations, boiler failure and dangerous late frosts. The whole operation required large amounts of labour at each stage, from the initial pot washing, barrowing of compost and seed sowing, to watering, pricking out, potting on, hardening off, and finally moving plants into position and planting out in the garden.

Opposite:
This portrait of Joseph Paxton by Henry Perronet Briggs (1793–1844) was commissioned in 1836 by his employer, the Duke of Devonshire, as a mark of respect for his favoured head gardener.

Matthew Balls (1817–1905) was head gardener at Stagenhoe in Hertfordshire.

Donald Beaton (1802–63) was well-known for his experiments in bedding design and contributed to the popularity of bedding as a fashionable feature of Victorian gardens. Beaton began his career in his native Scotland, working on a private estate near Forres before joining a nursery in Perth, and then working in the gardens of the Caledonian Horticultural Society in Edinburgh. He travelled south and was employed in private gardens, and in the 1830s began working at Shrubland Park in Suffolk, where he developed his bedding schemes. Dismissing new ideas on complementary colour theory, he advocated the shading of similar colours,

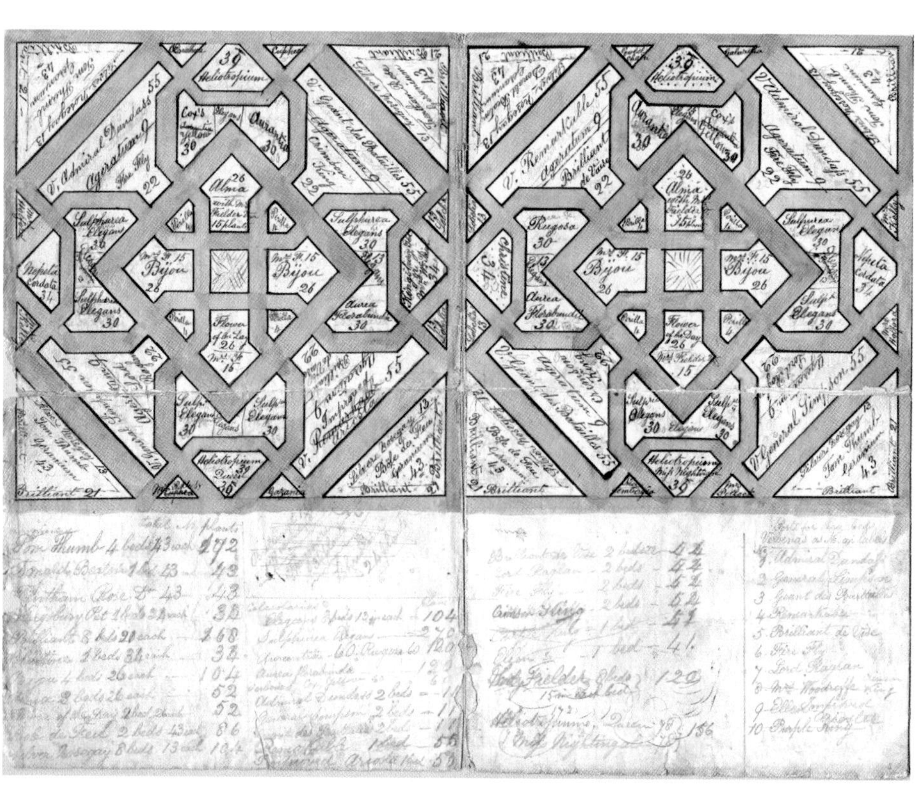

This bedding plan, designed by Matthew Balls for the gardens at Stagenhoe, indicates the complexity of design and the number of different plants required to create a summer bedding display.

planted to blend into one another to produce a sophisticated result that took into account a gardener's empirical knowledge of the effects of light and shadow, of daylight in differing atmospheric conditions, and of the influence of green leaves between the coloured flowers. His ideas were publicised through articles in *The Gardener's Magazine* and a weekly column in *The Cottage Gardener*, and his theories were tested in his acclaimed designs at Shrubland Park.

As the debate over bedding continued in the pages of the horticultural press, Beaton's colour innovations were spurred on by his friendly rivalry with fellow head gardener George Fleming (1809–76), working from 1841 at Trentham Park in Staffordshire, where he was famous for his long ribbon borders (see overleaf). A near namesake with innovative ideas on bedding design was John Fleming (1822/3-83), head gardener at Cliveden in Buckinghamshire from 1855. He trialled the use of spring bulbs in bedding displays and incorporated foliage plants as well as flowers in his designs. The culmination of his experimentation came in 1870 when *The Gardener's Chronicle* published a report describing Fleming's innovative design for a patterned bed of dwarf foliage plants and succulents incorporating his employer's monogram. This smooth, flat, closely patterned style of planting, named 'carpet bedding', was imitated in gardens around the country, incorporating heraldic devices, pictures, patterns and mottoes, and provided an opportunity for head gardeners to take horticultural artistry to a new level.

Annual bedding plants were bred by nurseries in a range of bright and contrasting colours, as depicted in an illustration from Carter's seed catalogue of 1898.

If an owner or head gardener had a particular interest or enthusiasm, such as cultivating orchids or ferns, they could specialise in collecting or breeding specific plants and gain renown for garden and gardener. The many new species being introduced to the gardens of Britain by plant hunters returning from exotic and unexplored countries provided opportunities for novelty and one-upmanship. Planting an avenue of the newly introduced monkey puzzle tree, or being the first to nurture a new species of lily into flower, would

Long bands of bedding plants in contrasting colours made up the ribbon borders at Trentham in Staffordshire, created by head gardener George Fleming.

propel a garden into the limelight, and a head gardener could enjoy an increase in his professional standing through such horticultural achievements.

John Gibson (1815–75) worked at Chatsworth under Joseph Paxton, who nominated him to travel to India on a plant-collecting expedition in 1836. He brought back forty-five cases of plants, among them over one hundred new species of orchid, and was rewarded for his success with a promotion to foreman of the exotic plant department. After seventeen years at Chatsworth, Gibson became the superintendent of Victoria Park in London; then, in 1854, he laid out a new park at Battersea. Using his knowledge of exotic plants, he experimented with subtropical bedding, creating the right growing conditions for striking foliage plants such as tree ferns and *Dracaena*. The effects were highly praised, and Gibson's innovative plantings were emulated in other gardens and parks.

William Barron (1805–91), head gardener to the Earl of Harrington, became known for his part in the creation of an extraordinary garden at Elvaston Castle in Derbyshire, which he began in 1830. Barron had served

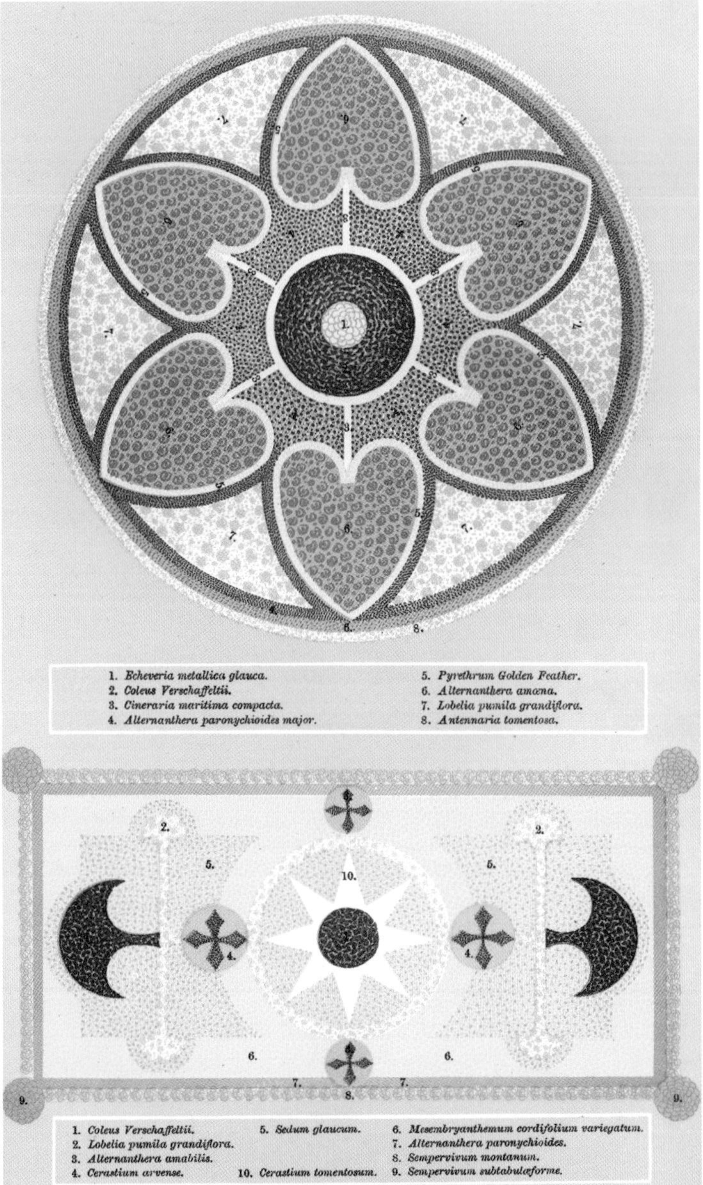

Head gardener at Cliveden, John Fleming's innovative use of low-growing foliage plants to create patterns like those on a carpet led to a new craze in bedding, culminating in complex three-dimensional figures and mechanical floral clocks. This design for carpet bedding was published in the *Gardener's Assistant* in 1888.

his apprenticeship at Blackadder in the Scottish Borders before continuing his training at Edinburgh Botanic Garden, and was then employed in stocking the glasshouses at Syon Park in south-west London. He spent the next twenty years creating a garden at Elvaston inspired by historic tradition and influenced by his employer's romantic tastes. The Earl's reclusive nature ensured that his remarkable garden was hidden from public view until his death in 1851; it was then opened to the public and caused a sensation. In place of the fashionable terraces of massed bedding there was a series of formal gardens enclosed by hedges displaying architectural topiary, fountains and specimen trees, inspired by the exotic gardens of the Alhambra and eastern tradition. He also created a pinetum and an avenue with multiple rows of trees of different species. All of this was reported to great acclaim in *The Gardener's Chronicle* in 1851 and prompted a renewed interest in topiary.

Barron continued to work at Elvaston until 1865, when he left to establish his own nursery and landscape gardening business in Derbyshire, where he was later joined by his son. His work at Elvaston had brought him renown in the transplantation of mature trees, for which he had developed a system allowing him to move large trees successfully over considerable distances, bringing an instant maturity to new gardens. In 1852 he published *The British Winter Garden*, which described the use of conifers to provide winter colour and explained his methods of transplantation. His innovative techniques and design flair, together with the publicity generated when the garden at

The extraordinary garden of Mon Plaisir at Elvaston in Derbyshire, created by head gardener William Barron, caused a sensation when it opened to the public in 1851. The garden is pictured in E. Adveno Brooke's *Gardens of England*, 1856–7.

William Barron developed a machine that enabled mature trees to be transported over large distances and successfully transplanted. A photograph of George Jackman of Surrey shows the machine in action in c. 1914.

Elvaston was opened, enabled Barron to develop his own successful business, trading on his horticultural reputation.

Head gardeners who were successful in the hybridisation of plants were able to enjoy the prestige that this brought in the horticultural profession while also enhancing the status of the garden in which they were employed. New cultivars of plants were sent to the Horticultural Society to be given the correct botanical nomenclature, which was often influenced by the name of the garden in which they were grown, of the owner or his wife, or sometimes of the head gardener who had raised the plant. This ensured the longevity of a gardener's reputation by recording his name in the annals of horticultural history.

The work of James Comber (1866–1953) is honoured in the new varieties of Rhododendron, Camellia and Magnolia he raised as head gardener at Nymans in West Sussex. Comber began working for Ludwig Messel at Nymans in 1895 after completing his training in a typically peripatetic style, beginning as a garden boy at Wakehurst Place in West Sussex, then moving to nearby Dencombe after three years, then a few miles further away to Tilgate Park as a journeyman for a further three years. In 1888 he gained experience at the celebrated Veitch Nurseries, and then was recommended by the nursery to work at Ashby St Leger's Lodge in Warwickshire, where he

The new species of Rhododendron and Azalea being brought to Britain by plant-hunters were extensively hybridised to create new cultivars. At Nymans in West Sussex, head gardener James Comber raised several new varieties.

was soon promoted to foreman. He then worked at Drinkingstone Park in Suffolk, before being appointed foreman at Longfield Castle in Wiltshire. Shortly afterwards, he was recommended as head gardener at Bignor Park in West Sussex, and two years later he began working at Nymans, where he settled and spent the next fifty years building the reputation of the garden.

At Nymans, Comber found soil that was remarkably fertile and a rich employer who was enthusiastic about plants. Together they created a pinetum, a rock garden and a heath garden, stocked the newly built conservatory, cultivated many rare plants from abroad, and experimented with hybridisation. Comber was paid well at Nymans and was provided with a large cottage next to the kitchen garden, in which he and his new wife, Ethel, lived for the rest of their lives. His horticultural achievements are remembered in the red Rhododendron 'James Comber'.

Head gardeners could also make a name for themselves by submitting articles for publication in one of the many horticultural magazines or by writing a book drawing on their experience or specialism. Having work published was a means to self-promotion and could gain horticultural renown as well as earning some money. Head gardeners could provide advice on cultivation techniques, recommend new products, review other gardens or instigate horticultural debate. Once a professional reputation had been achieved, founded on a combination of horticultural success and self-promotion, a head gardener might then be invited to become a judge at a flower show or to join the editorial board of a gardening journal. Apprentices would be keen to work under him, his advice would be sought by colleagues, and his employment prospects would be enhanced.

Rewards could also come in the form of certificates, medals and prize money. Horticultural shows were established up and down the country by local societies, and keen gardeners vied with one another to produce the best vegetables, fruit and flowers. The most prestigious shows were held in

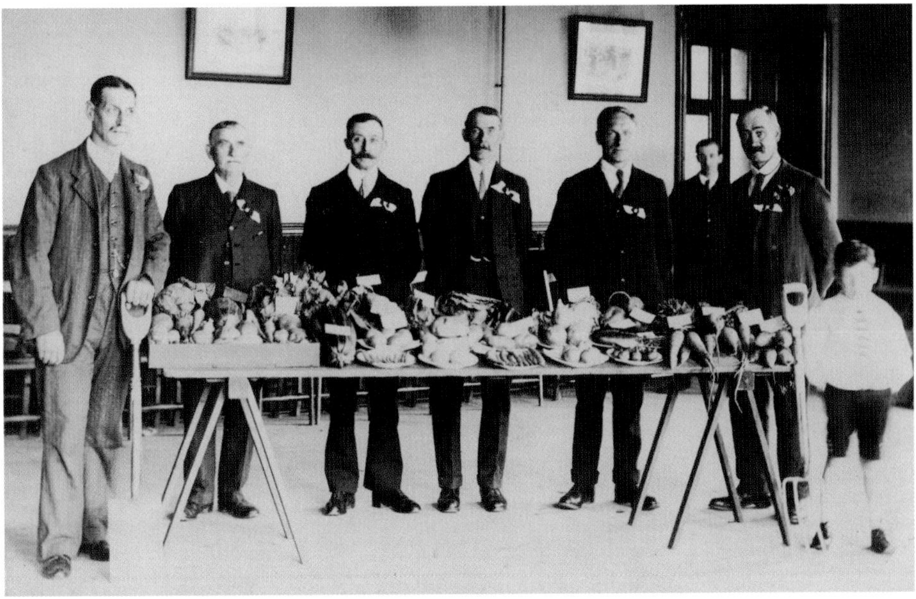

The awarding of prizes at horticultural shows was a serious matter, and being invited to judge the exhibits signified the high professional status to which many head gardeners aspired. This photograph dates from c. 1905.

London, organised by the Royal Botanic Society at Regent's Park and the Horticultural Society at Chiswick, later moving to Kensington. These shows gave head gardeners the opportunity to compete against the horticultural elite, matching themselves against the celebrated Veitch Nurseries or distinguished aristocratic gardeners, as well as measuring up to their most illustrious contemporaries. Although the prizes were awarded in the name of the garden owner, a head gardener would often reap rewards in terms of heightened professional status among his peers or the increased favour of his employer. Formal recognition of achievement was bestowed in awards such as the Veitch Memorial Medal, established in the 1870s to reward outstanding contributions to the science and practice of horticulture, and the Victoria Medal of Honour, first awarded by the Royal Horticultural Society in 1897 to mark the Queen's Diamond Jubilee.

James Barnes (1806–77) built up a considerable reputation in the horticultural profession through his successful cultivation of many rare plants and his exacting standards, but his fame rested mainly on the cultivation of pineapples. It was acknowledged among gardeners in the nineteenth century that the pineapple was the most difficult plant to propagate and nurture to produce fruit in Britain, and any gardener able to achieve this was highly regarded in the profession. At the invitation of John Loudon, Barnes wrote a series of twenty-four articles for *The Gardener's Magazine*, beginning in 1842, sharing his cultivation methods and horticultural expertise.

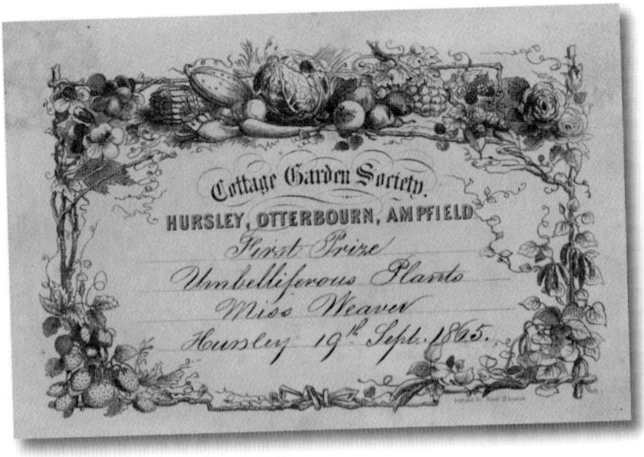

At horticultural shows gardeners could gain recognition among their peers for their achievements, although certificates were awarded in the name of the owner of the garden rather than the head gardener.

Barnes began his gardening career aged five, weeding and scaring birds with his father, who was a gardener, and he was officially apprenticed to him at the age of eight. By the time he was twelve, he had secured work in a London market garden, and over the next few years he worked in several market gardens in the capital, where he became a specialist in the cultivation and breeding of cucumbers. After working as a head gardener in Surrey, Essex and Kent, Barnes was appointed head gardener in 1839 to Lord Rolle at Bicton in Devon. After many successful years at Bicton, Barnes left in 1869 following a disagreement with his employer. He claimed he had been badly treated by Lady Rolle, who set out to tarnish his reputation when he became ill through overwork and was no longer able to carry out his duties. Barnes successfully sued his employer for libel and was awarded £200 in damages, emerging with his reputation intact and upholding the professional standing of gardeners.

The relationship between head gardener and employer was integral to the successful management of a garden. Joseph Paxton (1803–65) rose through the ranks of the gardening profession, using his talent, determination and ambition to achieve a knighthood, a seat in Parliament, considerable wealth and a distinguished reputation. This was all made possible through the horticultural affinity and mutual respect he shared with his employer, the Duke of Devonshire, at Chatsworth House in Derbyshire.

Paxton was of humble birth – his father was a farm labourer, who died in 1810 when Paxton was only six years old – and he followed his elder brother into gardening, working as a garden boy at Battlesden Park in Bedfordshire. He was then apprenticed to William Griffin, the head gardener at Woodhall in Hertfordshire, who encouraged the young Paxton in his horticultural career. After three years of training he returned to Battlesden and then, following the death of his mother in 1823, he decided to seek his fortune in London. He was soon appointed as a trainee gardener at the Chiswick garden of the Horticultural Society, where he was promoted after a year to under-gardener in the arboretum, cultivating the new species of trees arriving from abroad. In 1826, while working at Chiswick, Paxton met the Duke of Devonshire and made such a favourable impression that the Duke spontaneously invited him to become head gardener at Chatsworth, increasing his wages from 18s a week to £65 a year, with a cottage provided.

Paxton had evidently proved his worth to the Duke, as three years later he was given the additional responsibility of managing the woodland on the estate as well as the gardens, and his salary had increased to £226 a year. By 1849 Paxton's role had expanded to that of agent for the entire estate at Chatsworth, controlling the accounts for the house, garden, woodland, farms, villages, schools and fisheries, amounting to around £26,000. His salary rose to £500 a year and he employed two assistants to help with the workload. Three years later he was earning £650 a year and the Duke rewarded him further by remodelling his cottage into a grand villa with a turret and large gardens. Paxton worked at Chatsworth until the Duke's death in 1858.

James Barnes, head gardener at Bicton in Devon, was regarded as Britain's premier pineapple grower, winning first prize for his pineapples at the prestigious RHS International Exhibition in 1866.

Much of the success of Paxton's career was due to his relationship with the Duke. Paxton was a loyal servant who, despite the inequality of their social status, became a trusted friend of his aristocratic employer, travelling abroad with him, organising his affairs and sharing his horticultural vision. The Duke's immense wealth and propensity for spending allowed Paxton to create a garden of ambitious splendour, with fountains soaring over 80 metres high, a huge glasshouse known as the Great Stove, filled with exotic specimens, an arboretum planted with rare trees, and a rock garden of magnificent proportions. A visit by Queen Victoria and Prince Albert was organised with great fanfare in 1843, and Paxton enthralled the royal guests with a spectacular firework display and lamp-lit tour of the Great Stove.

Paxton's artistic and engineering feats in the garden were matched by his horticultural achievements. In 1836 Paxton caused a sensation when he exhibited *Musa cavendishii* at the Horticultural Society, the first banana plant to fruit in Britain, and then in 1849 he succeeded where others had failed by producing a flower from the magnificent giant waterlily, *Victoria regia*. Paxton's talents extended to architecture and structural engineering, demonstrated by his design and construction of the Great Stove at Chatsworth, completed in 1840. This complex glazed building employed over five hundred workers, who constructed 40 miles of sash bars to enclose

The Great Stove at Chatsworth was designed by Paxton and completed in 1840 at a cost of over £36,000. The conservatory was filled with temperate and sub-tropical plants, the impressive display prompting Charles Darwin to declare that 'Art beats nature altogether there'.

the sheet glass panes, and incorporated underground tunnels to facilitate deliveries of coal to the eight boilers, providing heat to the glasshouse through 7 miles of pipes.

The success of the Great Stove prompted private commissions for glasshouses from some of the Duke's friends, and Paxton was also the architect of several country houses, despite his lack of formal training. He designed Mentmore in Buckinghamshire, an eighty-room mansion completed in 1855 and complemented by an impressive garden, for Baron Meyer de Rothschild, and he worked on other projects for the Rothschilds in France. He also received commissions for public parks, beginning with Prince's Park in Liverpool in 1841 and Birkenhead Park in 1843, before going on to design other parks and cemeteries around the country, while still fulfilling his demanding role at Chatsworth.

Paxton is best remembered for his design for the Crystal Palace, which housed the Great Exhibition of 1851. Building on his experience of glasshouse construction, he created a vast cast-iron and glass structure of grand proportions, which complemented the British industrial and artistic achievements displayed within. The exhibition attracted over six million visitors and, when it closed, the building was dismantled and moved to Sydenham, where Paxton designed an impressive garden around it for the enjoyment of the public. Joseph Paxton was now a household name, and he was rewarded for his endeavours by the Queen, who bestowed a knighthood on him at Windsor Castle in 1851. His reputation was further enhanced when he was appointed Justice of the Peace for Derbyshire in 1853 and then elected MP for Coventry in 1854, and he served on the boards of the railway companies in which he invested his increasing fortune. He was a fellow of the Linnaean Society, an honorary fellow and vice-president of the Horticultural Society, a member and vice-president of the Royal Society of Arts, and an associate of the Institution of Civil Engineers.

Alongside his political, architectural, managerial, social and familial duties, Paxton maintained his professional standing in horticulture and published articles on gardening and a monograph on dahlias. He also founded *The Horticultural Register* in 1831, *The Magazine of Botany* in 1834, and *The Gardener's Chronicle* in 1841, all of which were affordable, accessible and aimed at the working gardener. Paxton had proved that through hard work, aptitude and tenacity, a labourer's son could penetrate the upper echelons of society through a career in gardening.

Paxton's Crystal Palace was moved to a new site in Sydenham when the Great Exhibition closed, and it became a popular venue for concerts, exhibitions and socialising, surrounded by spectacular gardens with water jets, carpet bedding and model dinosaurs.

FURTHER READING

Anthony, John. *Joseph Paxton*. Shire, 2002.

Bennett, Sue. *Five Centuries of Women and Gardens*. NPG, 2000.

Brown, Jane. *The Pursuit of Paradise: A Social History of Gardens and Gardening*. Harper Collins, 2000.

Campbell, Susan. *Walled Kitchen Gardens*. Shire, 2006.

Colquhoun, Kate. *A Thing in Disguise: The Visionary Life of Joseph Paxton*. Fourth Estate, 2003.

Elliot, Brent. *Victorian Gardens*. Batsford, 1986.

Hadfield, Miles. *A History of British Gardening*. Penguin, 1985.

Hadfield, Miles. *Pioneers in Gardening*. Bloomsbury, 1996.

Hobhouse, Penelope. *The Story of Gardening*. Dorling Kindersley, 2002.

Horwood, Catherine. *Gardening Women: Their Stories from 1600 to the Present*. Virago Press, 2010.

Ikin, Caroline. *The Victorian Garden*. Shire, 2012.

Musgrave, Toby. *The Head Gardeners*. Aurum Press, 2007.

Quest-Ritson, Charles. *The English Garden: A Social History*. Viking, 2001.

PLACES TO VISIT

Bicton Gardens, East Budleigh, Budleigh Salterton, Devon EX9 7BJ. Telephone: 01395 568465. Website: www.bictongardens.co.uk

Biddulph Grange, Grange Road, Biddulph, Stoke-on-Trent ST8 7TZ. Telephone: 01782 517999. Website: www.nationaltrust.org.uk/biddulph-grange-garden

Bodnant Garden, Tal-y-Cafn, Colwyn Bay, North Wales LL28 5RE. Telephone: 01492 650460. Website: www.nationaltrust.org.uk/bodnant-garden

Chatsworth House, Chatsworth, Bakewell, Derbyshire DE45 1PP. Telephone: 01246 565300. Website: www.chatsworth.org

Cliveden, Cliveden Road, Taplow, Maidenhead, Berkshire SL6 0JA. Telephone: 01628 605069. Website: www.nationaltrust.org.uk/cliveden

Cragside, Rothbury, Morpeth, Northumberland NE65 7PX. Telephone: 01669 620333. Website: www.nationaltrust.org.uk/cragside

Elvaston Castle and Country Park, Borrowash Road, Elvaston, Derby DE72 3EP. Telephone: 01629 533870. Website: www.derbyshire.gov.uk/elvaston

The popularity of amateur gardening was met with many practical products marketed at both men and women.

Garden Museum, Lambeth Palace Road, London SE1 7LB. Telephone: 020 7401 8865. Website: www.gardenmuseum.org.uk

Gawthorpe Hall, Burnley Road, Padiham, Lancashire BB12 8UA. Telephone: 01282 771004. Website: www.nationaltrust.org.uk/gawthorpe-hall

Hughenden Manor, High Wycombe, Buckinghamshire HP14 4LA. Telephone: 01494 755565. Website: www.nationaltrust.org.uk/hughenden

Kelmarsh Hall and Gardens, Harborough Road, Kelmarsh, Northampton NN6 9LY. Telephone: 01604 686543. Website: www.kelmarsh.com

Nymans, Handcross, near Haywards Heath, West Sussex RH17 6EB. Telephone: 01444 405250. Website: www.nationaltrust.org.uk/nymans

Peckover House and Garden, North Brink, Wisbech, Cambridgeshire PE13 1JR. Telephone: 01945 583463. Website: www.nationaltrust.org.uk/peckover-house

Rowallane Garden, Saintfield, Ballynahinch, Co. Down BT24 7LH. Telephone: 028 9751 0131. Website: www.nationaltrust.org.uk/rowallane-garden

Royal Botanic Garden, Kew, Richmond, Surrey TW9 3AB. Telephone: 020 8332 5655. Website: www.kew.org

Scotney Castle, Lamberhurst, Tunbridge Wells, Kent TN3 8JN. Telephone: 01892 893820. Website: www.nationaltrust.org.uk/scotney-castle

Standen, West Hoathly Road, East Grinstead, West Sussex RH19 4NE. Telephone: 01342 323029. Website: www.nationaltrust.org.uk/standen

Sunnycroft, 200 Holyhead Road, Wellington, Telford, Shropshire TF1 2DR. Telephone: 01952 242884. Website: www.nationaltrust.org.uk/sunnycroft

Trentham Gardens, Stone Road, Trentham, Stoke-on-Trent, Staffordshire ST4 8JG. Telephone: 01782 646646. Website: www.trentham.co.uk

Tyntesfield, Wraxall, Bristol BS48 1NX. Telephone: 01275 461900. Website: www.nationaltrust.org.uk/tyntesfield

Waddesdon Manor, Waddesdon, near Aylesbury, Buckinghamshire HP18 0JH. Telephone: 01296 653226. Website: www.nationaltrust.org.uk/waddesdon-manor

Victorian innovation was applied to gardening products, such as this patented rubber hose pipe.

INDEX

Page numbers in italics refer to illustrations